I Would Like to Say Thank You

JOSEPH DANDURAND

I WOULD LIKE TO SAY THANK YOU

poems

NIGHTWOOD EDITIONS
2025

1 2 3 4 5 — 29 28 27 26 25

Nightwood Editions
P.O. Box 1779
Gibsons, BC V0N 1V0
Canada
www.nightwoodeditions.com

COVER ART: Elinor Atkins (Miməwqθelət)
COVER DESIGN: Libris Simas Ferraz / Onça Publishing
TYPOGRAPHY: Rafael Chimicatti

Nightwood Editions acknowledges the support of the Canada Council for the Arts, the Government of Canada, and the Province of British Columbia through the BC Arts Council.

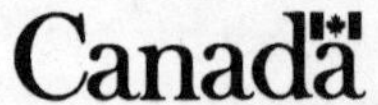

Canada Council for the Arts
Conseil des Arts du Canada

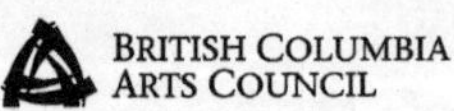

This book has been printed on 100% post-consumer recycled paper.

Printed and bound in Canada.

LIBRARY AND ARCHIVES CANADA CATALOGUING IN PUBLICATION
Title: I would like to say thank you : poems / Joseph Dandurand.
Names: Dandurand, Joseph A., author
Identifiers: Canadiana (print) 20250206099 | Canadiana (ebook) 20250206102 | ISBN 9780889714908 (softcover) | ISBN 9780889714915 (EPUB)
Subjects: LCGFT: Poetry.
Classification: LCC PS8557.A523 I86 2025 | DDC C811/.54—DC23

CONTENTS

My flow of inner life

I awaken from a dream where a large tree is falling
perhaps an omen of death to come and we wait
to see who is next as I have been to hundreds of funerals
each one sadder than the last and we bury the poor soul
we say goodbye and another tree falls and crashes
into the ground and life and death carry on
when it rains on a sunny day you could say
there will be a fight in the village and an uproar
that will settle down and we will go back to normal
if the frogs are singing it is time to break out
the drums and the blankets and start the fires
worship our spirits and keep them going
for the winter and when frogs start singing
in the spring it is time to get ready to fish
and worship the river and when the river rises
it is time of floods and worry and when the river drops
it is summer time and the summer fish are coming
and when a crow cries out there may be a birth
of a new child in the village this year we had seven
new ones born into this world of ours and when an eagle
whistles it is time to rest and take care of the sick
make sure they are comfortable make sure they have
enough blankets and when the sun rises
and turns a soft red it is time to say goodbye
and get ready for the next falling tree

I would like to say thank you . . .

to the nuns and priest
who abused me when I was six
thank you for doing that to me
and if you would like to see how I am
just look out your window
as I pass by because I know
where you live you old man

to the sisters I would like to thank you
for toughening me up for later in life
it was needed as I shook off all comers
I took the pain you gave me when you
stepped on my six-year-old brown hand
and told me to be still, God was watching

when I finally confronted
that old man I slapped him
across the face and in his eyes
I could see the lust he had
for me those decades before
now he weeps as the pain
in his face changes and I walk
away still that little brown boy
in need of comfort and I know
that I am who I am
and to you abusers
you cannot have me
you cannot destroy me
I can do that all by myself thank you

to the men who used me
when I was nine or ten
thank you for scaring me
and giving me nightmares
as they still haunt me here
at fifty-six in my little office
where I punch out poems
to soothe the soul where
I can relive the torture
of being touched by men
thank you I will visit one day
to slap you kick you bite you end you

the music changes
in my new headphones
I can hear the greats
and times when I was fifteen
drinking and doing LSD
and tripping in a bar
watching a Pink Floyd cover band
the bar lit with very cool lights
and I was tripping
and when it was over
the house lights came on
and it was then I realized
the bar was full of patched
outlaw bikers and there I was
fifteen and long haired and brown
skinned and tripping

but they let me float out
of there into the streets
me and my friends also tripping
we floated home and I am here
now putting on some blues
and writing poems
about this or that

I wanted to say thank you
to all the girls I knew
when I was fourteen
we all hung out on weekends
doing our best to be
as drunk as we could
and there were also gentle moments:
I remember being with a girl
and we made love and giggled
those around so wasted
they puked and pissed themselves
and we still conquered our teenage years
even today I remember each girl's name

thank you for loving me
when I was fourteen and skinny
and brown and long haired
not even sure I liked myself
and not sure I do now
the edges creepy
the hair gone

the eyes crooked
so is the nose
I weep myself
to write a poem
even though
I know
I have
been
forgotten

Voices driven to whisper

When there are stars in the sky
they say the fish are coming into the river,
so we as a people would get ready
to await the call to the fish and throw
our nets into the water and wait
for them to begin to shake.
When we were done our drift
we would pick the net up
shake the fish out and put them on ice.
When the net was in
we would repeat. This has gone on
since time began and we first fell
from the sky and landed on this island.
The books of history are all wrong,
only written to fit themselves
and their history even though
we were here before them.
They like to freeze us in time
and look at us as more of a nuisance.
We look at them the same way.
There was a time when
some of our young men
wanted to destroy them
and our elders told them
to leave them alone,
but they burned down that first fort
and now their new one
sits across from us. They claim
we followed them for protection

but we have always been here,
since we fell from the sky.
And so when there are stars
in the sky, get ready and go fishing
for the summer fish. Make sure
you get enough for the winter.
Make sure you are proud,
that you know who you are.
Do not let any old book
tell you different, and if it does
laugh at them and tell them
in your language that we should
have destroyed them
as they came to destroy us
through pages in a book about history.

Some endless hurt

Three eagles sit perched
upon a very large cotton tree
in front of my home
they stare at the emptiness
of this time and place
and I stand out there with them
and stare out into the drawings
from an old book
a great black book given to us
so we would be saved
and saved we are
as we all sit here perched
upon a great cotton tree
gripping the branches
with our sharp talons
and lighting the book on fire
watching her burn
as the eagles lift off
and pick up some wind
gliding into the path
of enlightenment

I am still standing there
as the big book burns
through all the lies and false gods
and we are saved from the church
that sits up the road
that no one goes to anymore
we should burn her down

to the ground where she belongs
as no one goes there to kneel
and repent and no one goes there
as the eagles soar above her
then land on the cross
each making room for the other
the three of them standing
on the cross as I watch
the final pages burn
and scatter into the clean air
of another Thursday morning
the final page lights up
and I catch some of the words
about a great flood
and how they survived
upon a ship made of wood
and the three eagles stand
there on the white cross
and stare down to see it
there it is for all to see
they begin to scream
and whistle into an old song
and the three of them
dance on the cross
and watch the ashes turn to dust
and I say a quiet *amen*
as the eagles scream

A shaming encounter

They say you will smell
a Sasquatch before you see them.
They smell like wet dogs
and it is good luck
when you do see them.

I teach this to children in the schools,
but am unsure if any of this is true
as I have never smelled a Sasquatch.
But lately I have been seeing them
—or images of them—in the ground
and in the trees and they never move.

This is perhaps why we never actually see them
moving or jumping or diving into the river,
but this does not quell the desire to see them.

If I ever did meet one on the street
or in the corner of a tree
I think I would ask them
if they are doing okay,
if they need a taste
of freshly cooked fish,

and if all the stories about them are true.
If the creature wanted a cold beer
I would walk down to the corner store
stand in line and buy a few cold ones.

After a few beers they would become comfortable
enough to speak to me about their life
and I would share my little life with them,
tell them that I too never wished to be seen
nor did I ever want the infamy of being a poet.

Then I would get a room,
a couple bottles of cheap wine.
We would sit and laugh and cry
and both of us would fall asleep

and in the morning the Sasquatch would be gone
and sitting there would be a note
and on it the words *thank you* and *see you later.*

I thought about this for years,
always looking for the beast
that I would never see again.

The room I sit in now
is full of rats and bugs.
Outside the city burns.
I sip on a warm bottle of gin,
I burn a smoke and talk to the beast
that is not there and never was,
but its scent lingers
and it smells like a wet dog.

Shattered

Inside this minute event of life
you can find me pressing
for more and more
of the eventual end
what of it and what about
all the trash I have seen
in my sixty years here on Earth
at first given a good little life
of a boy but soon
that was torn away
with abuse and beatings
and hatred of my skin
how did I deal with it
but the wrong ways of course
drink and drugs and
fights and violence

I made it to twenty-six
a drunk and addict
then woke one day
and said fuck it
I want to live
I want to write

And so it began
thirtyish years ago
on a dark winter day
out East on the coast

where I sat in a room
and chopped out
good and bad poems

This morning I do the same
but I have seen the wars
have won and lost love
have my three kids
we laugh as there is
no anger in our home
and here I am
a shatter of a man
who splinters into
many unconnected pieces
and if they get the time
to put me back together
I will be crooked and bent
and I will speak a language
of gibberish and will not
know enough to put one foot
in front of the other
and with the left and the right
I stumble into ashes
again aware of war and hatred
the demon of myself
only myself to blame
as I sit here in a world
where the stars glow
and sparkle the night

When I go outside I light a smoke
and turn the radio on loud
and drive into the abyss of make-believe
it is here I watch the sparrow and the crow
laugh at me and my broken wing

The little man told me

There forever am I
a piece of dust
or a piece of shit
depending how well
you really know me
and if we met
when I was younger
I was much more of an asshole
than I am now
as I fade into the sixtieth year
of this total waste of time
I have called my life
even though I have succeeded
as a father of some sort
if you will I can still feel
the strange murmur
of a loaded gun to my head
and temple and if the trigger
finger could just relax
I would splash my useless brain
upon the kitchen floor
and let the dogs lick it up
but if I was such a tragic manic-
depressed patron of drugs
and booze you could find me
floating downtown
in an old piss-smelling bar
with a lady on my hip
and we would be both holding

the other up and singing
bad tunes from the seventies
mixed with our prophetic speech
of mindless babble
on how we would change the world
if we could just find it
and if you see me on a stage
and I am the star attraction
please pay your fee and sit quietly
and do not interrupt me
as I have so much to share
with you and there may even be
a gem of a poem hidden somewhere
inside me but we all know
I was good in the past
and now the phone sits idle
and no one gives a shit
about an old poet really
because what the fuck
does he have to say
if he has not already said it before
and if you see me
on the river with a rock
tied to one of my legs
do not call out
leave me be to my escape
from all this
I know you do not see
what I see and I do not see

what you see but let's call it
a tie game and move on
and if you see me
jamming a needle
into my neck
just leave me be
in the alley
and go about your chores
and leave me be
to melt back into the sidewalk
and if you see me
please tell me you love me
as I am just a little boy
who was beaten up early
and told he was loved
and if we meet in a dark room
leave the lights off
as I am quite shy

Warm yellow moon

Give to me an old-time religion
and I will spend my days working
for the god you have chosen for me.
I will pray the fish will be coming back
this year in good numbers,
just enough so I can fill my freezers
and have some fresh fish to gorge on
as I rise up with Christ or whoever
they have awakened to pay the price
for freedom and salvation. I will walk
beside the chosen and I will hold
his hand and wash his feet.
Within this parable all will be healed
and my people will no longer suffer
as they have for a century now.
And when they took my mom
she was five and they sent her
to an old island far away,
and when she came back
there was nothing here
except the bottle and the abuse.
And so she left when she was eighteen
and never came back
until eight years ago, still drinking.
I told her she had to stop and she did.
She awoke and shared her story
to children, and she was more a saint
than any of those painted on the ceiling.

As I walk with Christ I ask him
a simple question: why did we
have to suffer if he had already paid
for our sins? And he never did speak
to me walking together to the promised land.
There we are, now, on an island
where we are waiting for the fish
to come back in good numbers,
and when they tell us we can go fish
we go at it hard and sleep very little.
We spend hours upon the river
fishing and fishing until the last minute
that was given to us, and the Lord comes
for a feed and we burn a plate of fish
for him and all our loved ones
who stand over there upon a hill
covered in old blankets, and God stands
there and eats the fish and he never says
a word to any of us.

Tell us about the bones

They found some unmarked graves
and it upset the world
but nothing was ever done about it.
Once someone raided
one of our old graveyards
and stole all the iron crosses,
someone even stole the bones
of one of our children.
I guess they needed them
for their cult or satanic beliefs.
We still bury our dead near there
at another graveyard located
right beside a busy freeway,
and my grandfather is there
with a few others of my family.
We keep the grass cut and gate locked,
and they have a graveyard in town
where a few of our folk stay,
and every year we burn
plates of food for our lost.

But who burns food for the kids
from all those wicked schools?
And who gives them blankets
as they are cold and lost?
And who feeds the missing
and the murdered?
And who shall place iron crosses
in their memory? And what of all

the extra bones found on that pig farm?
And who buried that pig farmer
when he was murdered a week ago?
Will he stay in the ground,
or will God pick him up
and toss him into the hell fires?

So, they find more kids in the back
of the schools of the wicked,
and how many more must we find
and take care of? Last week
we took care of my mom,
but she wanted to be cremated,
so we have her ashes.
We keep her warm and fed.

And what will happen for me
when I choose to go to the other side?
I think I wish to be also burned
to dust. You can scatter me
upon the river and make sure
you burn a plate of fish and rice for me,
and maybe an extra blanket
as there are those over here
who are cold and missing.

Statue of a dream

Some Nick Cave plays in the back of the room and I am at ease this morning though my guts have been bugging me for days because there are certain foods I need to keep away from but this morning the coffee tastes good and the weather is warm but wet from the western rains and the birds chirp and hop around the ground and the trees are full and green and there goes a coal train in the distance and the world is calm but I am sure there is war and destruction somewhere and our people have been on this island for at least ten thousand years and we are still here and I am here I am from here and my bones will stay here when they put me away and we still practise our ways which are old and there is no book and there is no wrong and it is based upon truth and the spirits give it to us and this is repeated over and over and we are still here and the pages of all the other books seem to seek war and they kill each other because they read and believe in another book and so we light a fire and we dance and sing and allow the spirits to join us and this is as old as time and when they found us and took us over they told us we cannot do this anymore and that we needed to read this big black book and so we read and we sang a few songs and learned to love the cross and the wicked teachings but this one day got old and it never did save us as we did not need saving and so we are now in our old ways and we dance and we sing and the words spoken are not from any book and we love each other and love the truth of who we are as the bombs fall somewhere over there where one book becomes another book and has nothing to do with the truth at all

Take me to your heart

I have had many lovers in my sixty years,
but now the bed I sleep in is empty
with no one to cuddle
or laugh with at how dumb I am.

It all began when I was seven
and fell in love. We played as friends
but nothing came of it,
my mind and body lost in love.
I can still remember her
as if she were standing
right in front of me.

Then in grade school
I had my first girlfriend.
She was nice and we still talk,
she far on the East Coast
and I on the West.
Back then, in high school,
there were many girls.
We all hung out as sort of a gang
from the south side of town.
We were all fourteen and started
in on the booze and drugs.
There I was with about ten girls.
I still remember today
as if they were standing in front of me.

And one night at a party
I met my lover, and we were
together for twelve years,
though on and off.
I punched out all the boys
she cheated on me with.

I, too, had other lovers,
but we stayed together through
the death of her mother,
who had brain cancer,
and her move down south
to be a nurse. I drove down
there and told her it was over
as I had found the true love
of my life in school,
both of us wanting to be actors.
I drove back and made it to the city
where I thought I would live
a long life with my true lover,
but it was then I realized
she had found her true love,
not me, so I punched him
in the head and came out West

where I met my wife.
We would have three kids,
but that marriage never made it,
though I was with her fifteen years.
She passed away three years ago.
I still take care of our kids.
It is me alone on a big bed
with one of my dogs,
who sleeps on the back of my legs.

And sixty years in
I still want to be loved.
I want to be cuddled.
I want someone to laugh at me,
tell me how dumb I am,
how dumb I was in this lover's life
of endless affairs. If I could
I would not change a thing,
yet here I am
and, if you want
an old man lover poet,
drop me a line
and I will come running to you.
I will kneel down
and devour you.

Way out west

Once I had a one-way ticket
from California to the North
I was alone and it was a lovely ride
and when we reached New Mexico
I was taken off the train and searched
as I guess I fit the bill of a drug smuggler
but alas I was just a lonely poet
and when I finally made it home
waiting outside my door
were some flowers from a lover
I never did find out which one
as I loved them all equally
and then I sat down and wrote
a new play and the next was my first day
at being the writer-in-residence
and they treated me like I was a threat
I made sure to take as much as
I could from them then left them
standing there as I'd had enough
of being treated like a crook

I drove my old car out West
and as I came down the mountains
I could finally see the river
gorgeous and flowing to the west
and I made it home where I sit alone
in a room at a desk the words pouring
out of my mind wishing for the touch
of a woman and to kiss her on the lips
I will slip my fingers into her softness
I will whisper in her ear that I am real
not a crook and my words are my words
and as we both become entangled
with lust I will enter her
and whisper into her ear
and she will moan
as the river flows to the west

Cycle

You could cherish the shortcomings
of a man who came into this world
when war and glory had lost its taste
and if this man was your father
you could forgive him for the beatings
and the words *I love you* afterwards
but I never could understand
or like my old man as he was cut
from a cloth of hatred and smoked
menthol cigarettes and drank
his undying anger catching me
in the corner from time to time
he would take off his thick black belt
and pull my pants down
the first two hits making their mark
then he would miss and hit himself
which pissed him off even more
and he would tire and light a smoke
and tell me he did this to toughen
me up and make me respect
what he called rules

When I had kids the thought
of hitting them was so foreign to me
so I guess I stopped the cycle
that is what I tell myself
that my old man was just repeating
what his old man did to him

to toughen him up but what it really did
was dull his senses and his empathy
and love and hate were all mixed up

I buried him a long time ago
when he died out East
right there on the living room floor
when his heart just blew
and when he was in his casket
I swear he was smiling
that mean prick of a man
who never did toughen me up
as I did that on my own
taking the beatings and abuse
and coming out a soft and humble
giving poet who can relive his past
and deal with it the best I can
and one day I will meet up with him
I will bring some menthol smokes
and we can look back and laugh
and tell each other that we love ourselves

Hearing my voice

They come to me in waves
of uncertainty from somewhere
inside a mind that likes to deceive,
likes to wander endlessly
into a vast valley of the unspoken
where I can sit for a few moments
to collect my thoughts
then run away to the hills.
I can get in my truck or get on a plane
and get the fuck away from the misery
that we call Reservation #6.
It is here that I wish to leave
to venture into the abyss of light,
and when I get there I never look back
as looking back is so futile
so I sit on a rock and listen for songs.
They come to me and I cry and I sing
them softly and sometimes it is when
I am on my boat and it is early morning.
I am waiting for the clock to tell me
it is time to throw my net out,
and when the clock is set I begin to back
my boat away from the shore
and throw my net out.
When she is all out, I turn the motor off
to drift down river and wait
for the net to begin to shake,

and when she does I race over
and begin to pull her up into the boat,
and there shaking and still trying
to swim upstream is a nice eight-pound
spring salmon, so I snap her out of the net
and put her on ice then release the net
and go back to one end and continue
to drift down river, and this is where
I wish I could be for the rest of my life.
But it too has its problems.
It is that I am all alone.
All I have is this fucking mind of mine
teetering on reality and conquered
by the deep depression that follows me
as I sink deeper and listen to the river
telling me that one day she is going
to cut me down and down I will fall
into her, falling deeper and deeper.
They say when you are drowning
there is a moment when you stop
struggling and you accept your fate,
and when that time comes I will be ready,
but for now I dream of escape
and the warm touch
of a flame made of reality.

Pale purple and bluish hills

I did a lot of acid in the eighties
and was so afraid of it
I would only do quarter hits
and be high all night long
I would stare at my hands
as they changed into
beautiful colours of the rainbow

We were only fourteen years old
getting high partying
drinking beer, smoking hash
when the acid high was over
you were so drunk you fell
into bed and spun around
the room, but today I am sober
and you can go to the corner store
and buy candy drugs
if you need needles
they will be provided

I have worked in the east side
where you can see the work
of hard drugs as men and women walk by
bent over stricken with bad dope
and the dealers keep dealing

The young come to the city
for excitement, and most get caught up
in the hardness of this world
and me, I am sober watching
the masses as they pass me by
I go and read some poems
to the street people
who love me and my words

I leave the city and the nighttime glare
of the rainbow of addiction
it is the screaming that gets to me
as I go home to my paradise

where I am glad my kids are sober
working hard as a family of hope
I pull into my driveway and open
the garage to walk into my home
I go to my bed and stare at my hands
for hours as the night lights glow
a deep yellow and orange

World Wide Web

I am like a spider as I throw my net into the river
and await the fish, but it has been a hard couple of years
as the fish are in trouble from overfishing and pollution
and the destruction of spawning grounds. And so I wait
for the King to say it is time to fish, and my boat sits in my yard
and my nets are ready and I am ready but the river is so low
as it has been for years now. And the weather has changed.
It is warmer, but we have taken the fish for thousands of years
and we have survived all the shit from the King and his followers
taking and putting us in their schools, but that one bit them
in the ass, and we never did change, and we are still here
on the river as the fish struggle. And I am one of the spiders
and I throw my net and watch it, and when it shakes
I rush over and pull out a nice twelve-pound spring perfect
for a meal. And tonight we eat fresh fish and rice
and some berries, and time repeats and history repeats
and the King far across the oceans sits on his throne
of tears and falls asleep as the spiders crawl over him
creating a nice warm blanket of web.

Doing the work

Heard this one in an old longhouse
where they still had open fires
and the air was full of smoke
we had been there thirteen hours
sitting on old planks
and my ass hurt
so did my back
but we sat there
to support the family
and the work they had on their minds
and the room was full of smoke
and people coughed and singers spat
people were even smoking
in that small room
it was an old home
and it was falling down
there were no washrooms
you had to piss in the bushes
they served a meal of fish and wild meats
we ate then sat for another four hours
and then the work began
that took another five hours
when the work was done
the family gave away all
they had gathered for four years
that took another three hours
then a speaker stood up
and the room got real quiet

he was from this part of the world
this was the home he was born in
and when he was a kid
he would listen to the old ones
telling stories and then he shared a story
about a crow who could see into the future
and all the crows loved him
and always went to see him
when they were near his part of the world
and this crow became old and grey
and one day all the crows of the world
gathered and they held a feast
and told stories
and the old crow stood up
and he spoke in his language
and he talked about rivers full of fish
and forests full of wild meat
he talked about how he fell in love
when he was young and his partner
had so many young ones
and how they both provided for their young
and he told us how one day his mate
became sick and so too did half his people
all stricken with red spots and fevers
he said he held her in his arms
until she took her last breath
and now he too only had a few more breaths
of air left so he walked into the fire

he turned to smoke and I heard this story
and my ass and back ached
but we stayed another thirteen hours
and the stories were glorious and ancient
and the smoke filled the room
and outside you could hear the crows
as they soared into the smoked-filled air
and sang songs in their own language

The widow's garden

Lovely flowers adorn the yard
and in the back she works
on some dirt and weeds
beside her sits her glass of wine
it is mid-afternoon
she is already pissed
chickens run around the yard
and in and out of the kitchen
she looks up into the hot August sun
the smell of fish guts in the air
as she had just cleaned thirty fish
given to her by one of her sons
the crows are the first ones there
to pick at the back bones
for the tastiest pieces
and she sips from her glass
and stands up about five feet tall
her hair long and black
she is in pain as her liver is dying
she has maybe a few more days
left on this earth and she lights
a joint also given to her by a son
she breathes in the weed
which helps with the pain
and goes back into her kitchen
to chase out the rooster
she shuts the door and sits down
in her small living room
turning the TV on to watch

her soaps and slowly fall asleep
it is nighttime by the time
she awakes and makes a piece of fish
and some rice for her dinner
as she eats she looks up to the wall
and there sits a picture of her children
all seventeen of them
she is near five feet tall
her hair long and black
and she eats and washes up
checks on the chickens
making sure they are in their pen
as the coyotes are on the hunt
the rooster snores and she shuts the door
goes up the old stairs to her bed
and she climbs in and turns the fan on
takes one more sip of warm wine
and she was my grandmother
a tough little woman
she never did make a few more days
as this was her last night
her son found her the next day
and he cried and later burned
that house down when he was drunk
and high on speed
and the rooster cried
for the morning sun
to erupt into laughter
of a mother and her children

Evasive explanation

We used to pray to God
because they told us
our ways were wrong and evil
and if we followed our old ways
we would go to hell
they made hell sound so bad
no one wanted to go there
so we kneeled
and listened to the stories
some sounding familiar
like the great flood and the fires
and the sickness we had suffered
—we survived all of those—
we never kept any of it in a book
no, we passed it down with words
and stories and we had saints
but called them healers
that were real, not made up
to appease anyone, and we even
had a place we would gather
and today we still gather
I am the fire keeper of our home
I open the doors and seat the guests
we feed them with a great feast
then we ask anyone who wishes
to speak to speak and share words
and teachings and when it is over
I check the fire once more
then lock the doors, and down the road

from us is an old white church
that sits silent and is one match
away from going to hell
but we do not burn her down
she sits there empty and we cut the grass
we even leave a few nice flowers
on the windows are painted scenes
of saints while our healers walk right past
they smile and see things we cannot see
they can see the dead whom we feed
plates of their favourite foods
the healers do the work
and can talk to the dead
to see what they may need
sometimes they wish for another blanket
or a cold drink and we give it to them
and the healers put the blankets
on the fires and they turn to smoke
the ones on the other side are thankful
and the old church sits empty
and the saints are starving
and they wish for a plate of food
but they have been forgotten
and now they sit within an old book
opened to the page about the great flood
then the page turns and lands upon
the story of how Jesus could heal the sick
and we have that one too
it happened just the other day.

To breed a storm

I burn three candles
taken from my mom's funeral
they sit upon my messy desk
along with me
the death of my mom
hit the kids the hardest
I took it all in and said little
let my brother make
all the right choices
we had seen it coming
Parkinson's wiped her out
she struggled to breathe
the nurse came in
and gave her pain meds
came back fifteen minutes
later she was gone
in a single breath
we took her to
the funeral home
they know us by name now
as we bury all our dead with them
my cousins and family carried her out
we drove with a police escort
back to Reservation #6
our old village
where Mom was born
1942 born in poverty
taken at five
to residential school

left this place at eighteen
joined the army
and met my old man
we lived away from here
but I came back
thirty years ago
a broken shell of a man
a lost lover
was going to stay and fish
never left and have worked
for my people
burned a life
and burned a mind
we carried Mom
out of our home
she was turned to ashes
sits on a ledge
beside my old man
sits on a ledge
next to a cat she loved
I breathe in
I breathe in

Faint symptoms of improvement

There were signs on the wall
there were signs from the animals
a small bird saw me and never moved
she pecked at the ground
searching for small snacks
searching for a few seeds of life
there were signs in the sky
the everlasting half of a moon
the lone star and the clouds of grey
no rain for a few days was a sign
the coldness of November
the ice on the dirt road
there were signs she was here
a lone deer across the yard
one eagle that soared to the tallest tree
she screeched and she whistled to me
telling me she was there
there were signs when we left the graveyard
the smell of rain and the smell of the river
she was there and we knew she was
there were signs that she was now gone
a spirit who had become a spirit

she was in the flames of the one fire
she was floating in the smoke
there were signs she loved me
I keep those stored somewhere
the fallen tears are somewhere as well
there were signs that I could have done more
there were signs that told me to be aware
I think I looked the other way
as we sometimes do

The dogs of the priests

There was an old photograph
on the shore of the river stood a priest
kneeling below him were small river kids
each one with their hair cut short
each one dressed in black
they did not look into the camera
behind them the trees were all gone
cut down to build the new school
built strong and ancient
it too stood on a hill above the river
this is where they took all the river kids
at age five they were sent there
some never made it past the first week
some went crazy and took their own lives
some tried to run all the way back home
they ran and ran along the river
it was cold and night had fallen
they found those river kids by the tracks
they buried them behind the cafeteria
where the river kids were fed mush
where the river kids starved slowly
some made it home and others were lost
some who made it all the way are still here
we thank them for their journey
they look at us with sad and hungry eyes
they remember the times when they were taken
when they were left in a room
where the rat-faced priest burned them
told them to take off their clothes

he liked boys
he liked young girls
he told them never to tell a soul
he told them God was watching
we look into the eyes of the survivors
the past in their eyes is there
the little river kids
the ones who did not run away
we love them
we cherish them
without them we would not be here
we the river kids
a new generation
never to kneel again
never to mouth the word
amen

For in his heart he hated

Images of war present themselves again
I grew up in fear of the mushroom cloud
born into the slaughter of a people
lived through a war so cold
watched the bombs as they fell
today is no different as the terror is here
we watch it from afar and we weep for them
the war here is quite different
it is almost silent but still deadly
they keep us on an island
they recognize us but they defy us
they keep our freedom and we are a number
5640010801 is who I am to them
a silent casualty of digression
they give my kids their own numbers
they are a new 564
a member of a race
the Kwantlen
the tireless
the bombs hit us years ago
shot from a wooden fort
built to begin the take over
today we are a number
the cannons aimed right at us
I await the mushroom cloud
we are just a number
5640010801

Guarded approval

I saw a bug who had crawled as far as it could
we are like that bug crawling forward
ready to end the last step
we try and try to be good people
some of us succeed and others fail
I am one who has failed miserably
left so many lovers in a state of confusion
had many lovers who left me standing there
left and never to be seen ever again
we made love in the candlelight
we made love in cheap rented rooms
we made love
now I crawl a little slower
my legs work at half speed
my feet hurt and my ankles burn
this is where I am now in the crawl
this is where we all are in the crawl
I left another lover
she died from pills and agony
I watched as they carried her away
my kids had just lost their mother
we all went and had a feast
each of us crawling out of the room
my legs no longer legs
they have become small and useless
I slither a few more miles
one day knowing it will end
the last step
the last crawl

The guilt must not be shared

Let us purpose the idea of a nation
It is quite simple but also deadly,
for there were a people already here
You acknowledge us before you eat
You accept the land was taken from us
Let us purpose the idea that we are a race
Our ceremonies were condemned by laws
The oblates almost shit their pants
when we would gather in our big houses,
dancing and singing for days and nights,
and at the end we gave it all away
The church blames us and called us heathens.
We were taken as children
A purpose to assimilate us to your goals
The land was taken and we were placed
We were placed on parcels of shit lands
Most of our lands today sit on floodplains
Some were lucky that we lived in old villages
Today our people are still here
Let us purpose that we are different

We speak a different language
We believe in a different god
We are small in numbers,
most taken by disease,
most brutally changed by schools,
but let us purpose that we are going nowhere
I am still here,
a man of a people
Let us purpose that I am a man
Let us light our little fires
Let us gather and sing and dance
We have been doing this for thousands of years
Allow us this one thing
as you acknowledge us
Thank you for your understanding
The purpose of this lament
is one for the ages

Deep black-green waves

Into the depths of the river I am waiting for her to appear and I wait a few days and I am growing tired of swimming and then she comes out of the depths and she has been to the ocean and she is now breathing fresh water and I swim up to her and I kiss her hard on the lips and she kisses me back and my tongue can taste the ocean and the saltiness of her life and we swim up river and we swim fast through the dangers of the water and we make it to a small waterfall and we rest a few days and then we make it further up past the canyon and we are almost home and we can smell our past and she slows as she has been in the ocean for four years and I too am slowing down and I flick my tail and make it past a mountain and she follows me and then we are home in the old waters where we both were born a thousand years ago and we do this every four years where we come home and we make a nice nest in the sands and rocks and then she smiles to me and we kiss hard once more and she then releases a million of her eggs upon the sandy nest and I follow behind her and I release my seed and it falls upon the ruby red eggs and then we both stay there for another few days and we both are beginning to break down and she is the first to pass over and there she is floating upon the surface and I have a few more hours left on this earth and I flick my tail once more and then I am gone and the eggs sit there and one day they begin to move and then they break free and they are the children of our love and then they begin to make their way to the ocean where they will feed and one day I too come back and wait for my love to appear and then there she is and we kiss hard

As if a transparent cloud enveloped me

The murky air glooms
into the depths of the city
where I have lived before
and do not miss much
because the dirt and piss
and other humans breathing
my air I can do without

If I do go to the city
it is only for a short time
usually to read poetry
so I park underground
in the darkness of a building
and walk out to the street
a few blocks uphill
then sit on a corner
watch the world go by

So many humans
to watch and remember
for use in future and past poems
I sit there and light a smoke
no one pays me much time
they get on with their hustle
get on with being humans
who can still breathe

For some even that is hard
there are those who are high
gone past the moment
they live one step ahead of us
and breathe in
we breathe in

I light another smoke
as I still have half an hour
before I am to read
I watch as the dirty men
and lovely women go by
some stop to buy weed
or smokes for a dollar
the dealers drink beer
in paper bags and winos
stumble over broken glass

Then there is a siren
an ambulance appears
to take one away to paradise
there are those who search the ground
for pieces of rock to smoke
they look down and pray
for a piece of heaven
but there is no more left
as the summer rains
have washed it all away

I finish my last smoke
cross the street and walk
into an ancient library
they greet me as the needles
fall upon the ground
I sit on the stage as they introduce me
I say hello make a few small jokes
and they laugh and I have them
as I read the first piece and I have them
I am their drug for the night
and when I am done I take their money
and make my way back to the street
walk the few blocks downhill
and find my truck and she is safe
no one has broken into her
so I start her up and make my way
down and out of the dirty building
fight the traffic and merge back
onto the freeway
I open all the windows
light a smoke and breathe it all
in the taste of death tickling
the tip of my liar's tongue

Cured of the shuddering heartbeat

The great moon rises in the east.
The sky is half full of stars.
I see and hear an old owl
on her way to the barn
where she has a nest,
where she feeds her young.
Night is when the spirits come out
to play, and they say you must stay
inside by three p.m., as that is when
they first walk out and begin their tricks.
They love to tease us here on earth.
You have seen them or heard them
in the thick forest; the owl leaving
the nest hunting for mice
and other things to feed her young,
three new ones to raise and to protect.
She glides over the valley,
stars lighting up the soft world.
She sees a mouse and down
she glides, her talons ripping
into flesh, and back up in the air she goes,
back to the old barn to feed
her screaming babies. And as the moon
drops down in the west,
the sun peeks out from the east.
Up she rises, and the owl sleeps
most of the day; the spirits hiding
and awaiting the moon. They look at all
the things they have stolen from us:
there is a sharp fishing knife

and some spools of red wool.
There is even a fresh fish
they have taken from a tote.
They eat the fish raw
with a few stolen potatoes,
then they too sleep the day away.

The moon reappears,
and the owl and the spirits
are on the move, the spirits
finding a bucket of fish heads
that they take back to the spirit world
where they boil them in hot water
and eat the eyes and cheeks
along with a bowl of stolen rice,
as the owl glides over the forest
and sees a nice-sized rabbit,
dives and jams her talons into the spine,
and she brings it home to rip it
into smaller pieces to stuff her new ones.
The moon rises and the spirits walk
around this island. They find old wine bottles.
They take a car tire and bring it back
to their world, and it sits there for centuries.
The moon rises and falls as all the stolen trinkets
gleam in the soft light of a new moon.

One-way roads

With every page of this book
there are reasons for the non-linear ways
if I may explain it simply
it is like having a mind that does not return
what is being thought of

It is like having thoughts from a map
of only one-way roads
and you never can get to the end of it
so you keep doing it day after day

You have accepted there is no end
so here you go, another trip
down memory lane of a mind
of a child who can only be normal
when telling a story about his past
as he gently shows you how he thinks
in broken channels
and the roads never end
so he keeps driving towards the eternal
sharing more and more
of what is left inside him

Here is another one for you
when you are done toss it away
like we do for all mindless images
here is another one about a time
when he was little and how some boys
tricked him and told him to kneel
and open his mouth
he was so upset and never told anyone
and the boys laughed
and later when that priest told him
to take down his pants
in a bathroom stall at a Catholic school
he never told anyone
and how he could not love his lovers
to the fullest as he was so sure
he had hardly any trust left
and if you wait long enough
if you turn the page there will be one more
childish picture painted for you
from a mind of a map
that only goes one way to the left
then turns to the right and falls close
to the edge but as it is only one way
you make it back and here now is another

Lifestyles of the rich and famous

The first time we met
it was love at first sight
or something like that
we both were to be famous actors
she fulfilled her dream
and I went on to suffer
the life of a poet
she was on TV
and I in a cold room
with a pen and paper

She spoke so well
and I spoke not at all
just through my many forgotten
books of poems
and she went on to marry
her true love
so I lost mine to another man
and another life
she had three kids I have three kids
mine are working for our people
all healthy and full of humour
they make me laugh
and we live on
and I live on with this constant need
of a lover who will never be found
so I write bullshit poems
about lost love

I still sit in a cold room
with a pen and paper
jotting down
small anecdotes of true love
how it should have been
how the affair we had at school fooled
everyone or so we thought
and people got hurt and I got hurt
when I left a life to join a new one
only to find out I had been replaced
months before and he was beautiful
I was nothing compared to him
so I punched him in the head
and called her a few dumb names

I walked out and drove for a while
then checked myself into a psych ward
where I ate toast and sipped tea
and smoked smokes and met God
and met psychopaths
and insanity at its finest
they were men just like me
so I ate until one night
God came to my room
and asked if he could touch me
so I punched him in the head
and left the next morning
and drove for days to the village
my mom was from

I was not going to stay
was just going to rest
on my way to the Deep South
into the old world
then I was given a job
I have worked and lived here
for over thirty years now
I am not going anywhere
and have loved a few more
but they too failed and here
I am near sixty and so alone
in a cold room
with a pen and paper

Come to my own morality

We played cards in the quiet room
of a ward of insanity.
I played against God and Jesus
and a man who thought he was a lifeguard.
He even had a whistle,
which he blew constantly.
This annoyed God
but you got used to it.

The lifeguard was a poor card player.
I took all of his smokes.
He quit and blew his whistle
and ran down the halls screaming
for everyone to get the fuck out of the pool.

They quietly took him to a happy room
covered in soft pillows
where he stayed for several hours.
When he was calm, they let him out
and he went right back to work.
I think he even saved someone
from choking in the kitchen.

And it was just me and God and Jesus.
They were both ahead of me,
but they were of course cheating.
I knew the scam was on,
and yet I stayed and did quite well
until the dinner bell rang,

and, like test rats, we stopped playing
and went and ate a meal
of mashed potatoes and a nice, thick gravy.

Then we all went out
for one more smoke before bedtime,
and God told me a story
about his first and only love,
how he had caught her cheating with Judas,
how he sliced that fucker up into thirty pieces.
Jesus joined us and never said a word.
I was worried about him,
as he had been there for years
and they would never let him out,
as he loved the taste of fire
and had burned some people in an old church,
caught running away screaming
that the devil made him do it.

We finished our last smoke,
said good night, and went to our beds.
I shared a room with a pervert
who liked to lick the walls.
He was licking away
when I came into the room.
Then lights went out
and the pervert stopped licking
and went to sleep and snored so loud
you could barely hear
the whistle blowing down the halls
as the lifeguard had found Jesus
hanging from ripped-up sheets,
the light catching his image
just right to look crucified.
The whistle blew and the pervert snored
and all I could dream about
was my freedom and a way out
of this fucking hell of a mess.

Constant amazement at his perfect being

He walked out of the woods a being of sorts and some call him Sasquatch but he prefers to be known as just a man and he turns into the most beautiful man on the earth and he is perfect standing at six feet and weighing about two hundred pounds with long black hair and his skin is perfect and he walks the train tracks into the city where he stands with all the other brown people on the corner of Hastings and Main and there he sips beer and smokes weed and drops a few pills given to him by a young girl who sells pills and is totally in love with him and she buys him beer and new clothes and they live for a time in a one-room shithole where she does everything for him and she even gave him a child who still lives to this day and the two of them make love on the creaky old single bed and the walls shake and the earth moves and when they are done they take a few more pills and go out and search for something stronger and they find the black tar needed and they go back to their room where they undress and sip cold beer and ready a hit of tar and she goes first and he follows and they stay like that for three days and then he wakes up and walks out and she never sees him again and later she has his child and it is a baby girl with deep brown eyes and a head of black hair and she raises that child the best she can on her own and she sells pills and she works the streets and one day she too does not return and they say she is one of the missing and the child sells pills but she does not wish to stay in the city so one day she walks out and down the train tracks and she comes to the woods where her father lives and she walks in and she becomes a Sasquatch and she is near nine feet tall with golden black hair and she has deep brown eyes and she finds her father and he is drunk beside an old tree and she walks up to him and hugs him deeply and he smiles and takes one more breath and is gone and she leaves the woods and she walks the train tracks and before she reaches the city she becomes an eagle and she opens her wings and she glides over the city and she searches for her mother who is lost and missing somewhere below

Of pale-blue shadows

I wonder at all the shadows
I have seen in my life
some of friends
who died way too soon
one a spiritual brother
who sold and did heroin
shot seven times
the bullet into his neck
dropping him to the ground
I carried him to his grave
and shoveled the dirt
that would finally cover his shadow

I have seen and heard
trains going by
some in the distance
of my home
some across the river from me

It is usually when I am outside
my home late in the early morning
burning a smoke in memory
of all the shadows I have seen
and I put out the smoke
and go back inside
the dogs sleeping
dreaming of chasing birds
and lost shadows
they snore and kick
and run in valleys of cedar trees

I have buried
way too many
family and friends
always asked to carry them
one last time
this is how it is in life
and death and the other side
where all the spirits live
and swim in cool pools
of mountain-fed streams

And we today we swim
in these same waters
and dunk ourselves four times
it is such a great feeling
when you come up
after the fourth dunk
you are alive and then
you see shadows flying
in the cedar trees
laughing at you
as you try and walk out
of the swimming hole
and you fall back in
and scream from the shock
of the cold and the sprits laugh
and fly around chasing
their forgotten shadows

Then after your swim
you get dressed
and this is the place and time
where you can truly talk
so we talk and laugh then run
down from the mountain
we enter our home
the fires are hot
then the drums begin to slam
a new shadow is born
and up into the air they go
and around the floor
they are carried
and as the door closes
I can see my old shadow
sitting in the corner
lighting a smoke
as the new shadow
begins to scream

A day of daze and conjecture

They found his footsteps leading
to the edge of the raging river
where the night before
he had walked in with his pockets
filled with heavy stones
the easiest thing he had left to do
as in the past he had walked to the bar
across the bridge and drank beer
every day with a few shots of whiskey
then back across the bridge he would
stumble home and sleep it off

And one day he took the bus
into the city where he lived
what was the rest of his life
to work mind-wasted labour
to get his cheque and cash it
at the corner store where
he could buy a case of beer
and a mickey of whiskey
with enough money left
for a room at the corner
of death and doom
in the heat of the summer
the city smelling like warmed piss
and cooking shit and the rest
of the world was on the streets
trying to survive the heat
and the pains of being alive

He would finish the beer
and walk out of his room
to make his way to a bar
deeper into the east side
of town where he would sit
in the corner sipping cheap beer
with a few chasers but the pain
in his belly was becoming
too much they told him
at the hospital that his stomach
was bleeding from all the booze
so he stopped for a while
and found crack and heroin
and loved both but his shitty jobs
could not cover the cost of the drugs
so he went back to booze
and was near the end of it all
as he sat sipping gin in a park
filled with ghastly pigeons
who looked more like rats than birds

When he was done drinking
he got up to go home
but another drunk came to him
and told him he owed him money
which was not true then the other drunk
kicked him in the guts and he went down
and woke up hours later and went
to the river his belly bleeding
choking on blood and parts of his guts
as it was over for him
as he went to the edge
his pockets filled with heavy stones
wading into the river raging out
towards the ocean he went under
and stood there breathing in
once more filling his bleeding
body with fresh water
and in a few minutes he was gone
found downriver near the mouth
bloated and no longer suffering
free to dance and sing and drink
in the spirit world where he stayed
for a few centuries but again he was done
and said it was over so closed his eyes
saw his love and she was there waiting
for him wearing her gorgeous red dress

Snippets of the ambivalent

A wonderous aria plays in the room and I have just finished a smoke and today shall be busy as my middle daughter's car has a slow leak in her back tire and I have to pick up my son from his girlfriend's and I am waiting for parts for my boat motor and we are awaiting what is coming down river from a great flood in a small river where a mudslide created a dam of sorts and it blew open two days ago and all the shit in it is coming our way and we are to go fishing on Saturday for six hours and I hope to catch a few and sell them for five dollars a pound and make back a few bucks from what I have spent this year just to be able to fish and I need to go upriver and buy some cheap gas and some smokes from a reserve about forty minutes away where I do not have to pay taxes on smokes and gas and then I need a shave and some ice for fishing and I need to clean out some totes to put the fish in when I come home and I just bought a new scale to weigh the fish by the pound and I hope all will go well on the river as I throw a new net hung for me by a friend just down the dirt road from me and in all this I need to be as sane as I can be and I need to rest when I can and this is what fishing season is like you go and go and you have a sore back and legs and your hands are swollen from pulling the net in and letting it out and you pray that you do not snag up on whatever may be lurking beneath the water and when the net begins to dance you rush over and pull the net up and hopefully you snap out a twelve-pound fish and times that by five dollars a pound and there you have sixty dollars back in your pocket and you drop the net and you light a smoke and you drift and drift into oblivion

Razor's edge of jeopardy

There were three of them
a man and two sisters
who worked the streets
and at the end of a night
would share a bed and room
where they would cook up
what they had earned

This went on for a hard decade
until one of the sisters suffered
and was taken to a hospital
to never leave as her siblings
watched her fade and fade
weeping tears of true sorrow
but they kept on living
and working the streets
until one day the man dropped
dead on the busiest corner
of the city as the masses
kept going stepping over him

The last sister was done
working the streets
done cooking up her pain
so she caught a bus
back home to her village
on an island on the river
where she found her mother
who welcomed her home
together they would travel

all winter to the big gatherings
to watch the spirits dance
she was doing much better
but was spiritually sick
so her mother gave her up
to one of the homes
where they saved her

Now she is in her eighties
and is always asked
to bless the floors
of all the homes
she wears all red
and dances and dances around
all the dirt floors
of all the homes
and when she is done
she sits back down
and remembers her sister
and this makes her cry
tears of happiness
and sorrow
mixed together

And when winter is over
the sister now in her nineties
works on some beading
and she loves to knit
loves to watch her soaps
loves a sweet cup of tea
never forgets the city
and she opens the window
to her small home and outside
little songbirds gather
and the old woman
throws them some seeds
they sing and sing
and she smiles for the last time
as the first snowflake falls
from the graceful sky

All those I know

I was sent to Catholic School when I was five
and on the first day I got in a fight
with a big bully who did not like my look
we went at it like cats then Mother Superior
told us if we wanted to punch
we could punch a brick wall and I did
as the bully wept I kept hitting the wall
even after the Mother told me to stop
then it was naptime and fuck if I could rest
I was wired and then it was lunch
and Mom had made me chicken noodle soup
and a peanut butter and jam sandwich
I ate it all then it was time to kneel
before God he was everywhere
and there were pictures of his son
always nailed to a cross then it was time
to go home I got on the bus and sat alone
as my sister wanted nothing to do with me
as I was trouble or trouble always followed
me and when I got home the old man
was waiting for me and with belt in hand
told me to stop fighting then beat me
I went to bed without supper
a punishment from my mom

the second day of school I hid near the river
and there I found wonderful flowers
and flying bugs in the millions
then the bell rang and I made my way
to our class which was in the basement

of this glorious school then it was naptime
I was so hungry as I had not eaten since
lunch yesterday and when it was time to eat
I devoured the soup and sandwich
then it was time to kneel and the Father stood
at the front and I envied the altar boys
and the ringing of the bells and all I wanted
was to be the bell ringer but I never made it
that far in religion as we stopped going
when I was nine since then I have never
set foot in a church to worship a man or his son
who still hangs from a cross where his hands
and feet are nailed with huge nails and his head
is sunken to one side and he has accepted his fate
but me I have not accepted a religion from a book
and my beliefs come from long before Christ walked
on sands and long before any bully came my way
so I do not kneel and I do not repent and it seems
to have worked for me and now my kids follow
our ways and they start the fire and welcome
the guests and the drums begin songs older than
any man who lives in the sky and me well I am eager
to punch any wall for as long as it takes

My dreams are mere figments

I kill the flame
the world awakes
to a Friday morning
waiting for the sun to rise
I will go upon the river
and work eight hours
bring home some fish
then do it all again
Saturday and Sunday
but I must await the sunrise
then I can get ready
so I sit here in my office
answer the mail
play a game of mahjong
this drains my brain
for a few minutes
then I go for a smoke
watch the sun begin to rise
I go home and hook up my boat
and trailer to my truck
put some ice on the boat
then head down to the boat launch
back her in straight
set the trailer in the water
just enough to get the boat floating
then I push her out
and toss my anchor on the shore
and pull the trailer out
park up top and lock my doors
walk down and get in the boat

start the motor up
she is cold but she starts and idles
and then I raise the motor and prop
up a bit as the water is low
I need to make it out of here
to the main part of the river
and go to the eagle's nest
back away from shore
and release the net
that I have spent
a few hours repairing
and out she goes
the day of fishing begins
then I sit there and light a smoke
and drift down river
away from my misery
and loneliness and here I am
upon the great river
she controls me
and my ability to catch fish
and I watch the net
then she dances
and I race over
to where she is dancing
and pull and pull her up
and there is a nice twelve-pound
spring salmon I snap out
of the net and throw in a tote
and the sun rises higher
and I go deeper to the place in my brain
where all my secrets are kept

Permanent expression of grief

Where the river hits the island and it swirls
there are the remnants of a sunken boat
tied to a float collecting debris of broken trees
and other treats from up above. The current is quick
and pools and spins without any mercy.
You have to be careful upon the river as she is in charge
and you are just floating on her. As the pools spin
into small whirlpools, you guide your boat around
the head of the island. You come around the corner
and slow down to rest. You still have half an hour
before the laws allow you to throw your net out,
so you wait and drift down with the motor off
as the other big boats begin their journeys further
upriver from you. One minute before the gods
and kings have given you a few hours to catch
some fish, then you see the other big boats below
throwing their nets out, so you back away
from the river's edge and, when your net is all out,
you give it a tug to keep her straight. Then you wait
and watch the net until you see it dancing
at the far end, so you rush over and pull up
an eight-pound spring salmon, and you start to smile.
As you know supper will be tasty. As you throw her
into a tote of ice. And she still is trying to swim home,
but she is yours, and you throw the net back as you drift
further downriver until you are at the end of the island
in a deep hole where you pull your net into your boat
to make sure she is sitting properly, so when you
throw her out again she will go out straight.
You look to the time and an hour has passed,

so you race upriver and do it all again.
When the net is out, you shut off the motor
and light a smoke and you sip some cold pop.
You are sweating as the August sun burns your soul
and the river waits for her moment to despise you.
All of a sudden your net goes down hard.
You know you are in trouble, and you try and try
to rev your engine and break the net away
from the hidden snag at the bottom of the water.
Finally she breaks, and then you straighten her out.
Then a fish hits at the other end, and you race over
to pull out a sixteen-pound spring salmon,
and you are sweating as the August sun does not forgive.
You burn and you sweat and this is fishing,
as if we have been doing this all of our lives.
You pull your net in, and she is broken in pieces
from the snag and the ripping, so you join the pieces
as you float further downriver. And when you are done,
you turn your boat northeast and open up the engine.
You fly back and check the time and you have two hours left,
and this is fishing, as if you know what the fuck you are doing.

The pages flip over

Again the cool rain is upon our island
where we have lived since the ice melted
that is a good story but I believe
we have always been here
since we fell from the sky

Some might argue with this
as their book says something different—
that we all came after the apple story
we were made by one man
and we should worship him

They tried to save us
from what we believed in
and if we did not change
then we would all go to hell

That one never worked here
we still have an old white church
that sits empty and no one
from here worships there

We all gather in our longhouse
in the wintertime and we dance
and sing and share words
that are so old and passed down
from before and they tell
the same stories of floods
and fires and disease
and I believe so strongly

in my spirituality
that no book could even
make me think otherwise

So the ice melted
and we appeared from the sky
and we found this island
where some of us still dwell
and I live here and built my home
twenty-five years ago
and it sits on the edge of the river
standing higher than the last flood
as we wait to see if we will be
allowed to fish the river but it looks
like the fish are in trouble
their numbers kept in some book
the pages filled with blood-
stained numbers and my boat
sits ready with a brand new net
I hope to throw and drift down
and not catch any snags
and have her torn to pieces
and people are already calling me
for fish but I have to tell them
that I do not have any for them
as I do not have any for myself
and my family and the pages
flip over and my home is mine now
two of my kids still living with me
three dogs and a cat who hates me

I turn the fan on and go to sleep
and the pages are now burning
in a protest and we can be found
on page 34 next to the stories
of floods and fires and disease

Gesturing clumsily with knives

She would come at me in the kitchen
blocking my way out
and accusing me of all the dread
man has ever done
since time began

She would threaten me
with the kitchen knife
and when I chose to not play
I would move her out of the way
once outside the door
she would scream at me
to never come back
even though the home was mine

When we married
I made sure never
to put anything in her name
and kept my bank accounts
and home separate from her
I would get in my truck
so angry and lost
driving into town
to rent a room
staying until
all had cooled down

I'd come home
because I had three little ones
and she never spoke to me for days

which was nice
this went on for fifteen years
and one day when I was properly medicated
and could see clearly
I told her it was time to leave
she did as she already had someone else
and I just wanted peace and quiet
and it came
and it took years more of hatred
for us to ever talk
and eventually we became friendly enough
so I took the kids to Mexico for two weeks
and the first week was just me and them
and she was to fly out the following Saturday
but died in her washroom
I got a phone call and had to tell my kids
they were so young and screamed and cried
I too cried for them
and we flew home the next day
and we buried her following four days
of our culture and teachings

It has been near five years now
and I miss her and still to this day
love her but time must move on
and our kids are grown up
each one working for our people
content and carrying on
and me well I died a week ago
or maybe it was yesterday
I am not quite sure of the date
but I think it was on a Saturday
after a phone call
deep along the sandy shores of Mexico

Yesterday's anger has finer edges now

There is a family fight here on Rez #6
and very much like every other rez
we watch it unfold and it mostly
happens at our big gatherings
it is too old and boring
to actually give a shit about
so I shut it out and shut out the ones
who proceed to upset us
as they are upset about something
in most cases money and power
I live a fine life and my kids
all work here for our people
I shut the poor losers out of my life
they whine and boo hoo
I can never give in to them
so they wait for the next gathering
they do not care if it is a funeral
or celebration they stand and speak
you can cut the tension
with a good sharp fishing knife

I shut them out and work for my people
which I have done for decades
when I first came here I never wanted
to live and stay here but I was given a chance
and I took it and I turned it into a career
so today I sit in my office and am at peace
and quiet and the rains begin and the river rises
and the sun is hiding and the moon has fallen
off the sight from here and here is Rez #6
where I shut the door and close the sadness
in a pool of water that spins to the east
and then I shut my mind and I am at peace
and peace is so glorious and angry
and it too puddles up outside
of my door that closes and creaks
and the rains fall as the river rises

The ghost that is strange came for tea

If all I had to do was think and be clear
as to what it is I am trying to say to you
then it would all be so simple
but for years now
ever since I started writing
I am always holding back
never saying what I truly feel
how dark it could be
how deeply ugly I feel
not only about myself
but about this world
all the wars and suffering
not only of my family
and the Kwantlen people
who have resided here
for thousands of years
but when I write a poem
I try to not hurt anyone's feelings
I try to not speak the truth
to kindly hide it in metaphor
and carefully selected words

If I was to be who I am
and how my mind really works
I would be hated and loathed
my books would never sell
nor would they be published
so I hide for fear of being discovered
the fool that I am
this has gone on so long now
when I first started I wanted
to be famous and well-known
I wanted the world
to accept me and desire me
next week I am to travel out East
they will fly me out there
and put me up in a hotel and pay me
and if they knew the truth about me
and how I am quite psychotic and depressed
so close to walking away from this
as I have always eventually walked away
from the boredom and repetition
of being called a writer
and what if I wrote what I am truly feeling
right at this moment
it would be carnage and hate and blame and desire
and finally the last breath of a man
who was nothing more than a little boy
with pants that did not fit
and one button missing
from his white shirt

ABOUT THE AUTHOR

JOSEPH DANDURAND is a member of the Kwantlen First Nation, located on the Fraser River about twenty minutes east of Vancouver, BC. He resides there with his three children. Dandurand is the director of the Kwantlen Cultural Centre and the author of several children's stories and books of poetry including *The East Side of It All* (Nightwood Editions 2020), which was shortlisted for the Griffin Poetry Prize. In 2021, Dandurand received the BC Lieutenant Governor's Award for Literary Excellence.